W9-BUK-341

This book belongs to

....

This is a Parragon Book
This edition published in 2006

Parragon
Queen Street House
4 Queen Street
Bath BA1 1HE, UK

Copyright © Parragon Books Ltd 2001

All rights reserved

Created by small world creations ltd
Printed in China
ISBN 1-40545-084-3

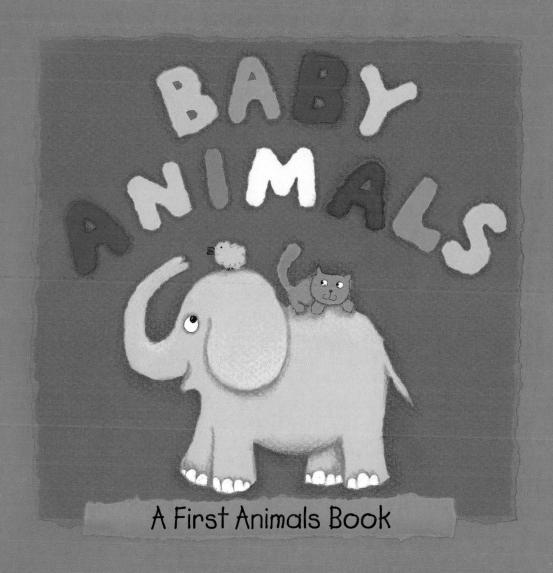

BABY ANIMALS

A First Animals Book

p

chick

Tap tap tap

the eggs crack

Cheep cheep!

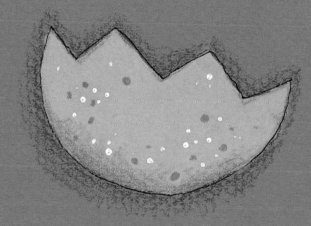

and out pop the tiny chicks.

kitten

New-born kittens are fluffy and soft.

and perfect for cuddling!

baby elephant

Baby elephants don't hold mummy's hand

when they go for a walk

they hold tails!

piglet

Baby piglets have
little pink noses

and curly-wurly tails.

baby bird

Sleepy baby birds snuggling

together in their cosy nest.

calf

This baby calf has black and white patches just like mummy cow.

lion cub

Baby lions are called lion cubs

and they have
very sharp claws.

lamb

Little lambs like to jump around

and leap high into the air.

puppy

Puppies love rolling round

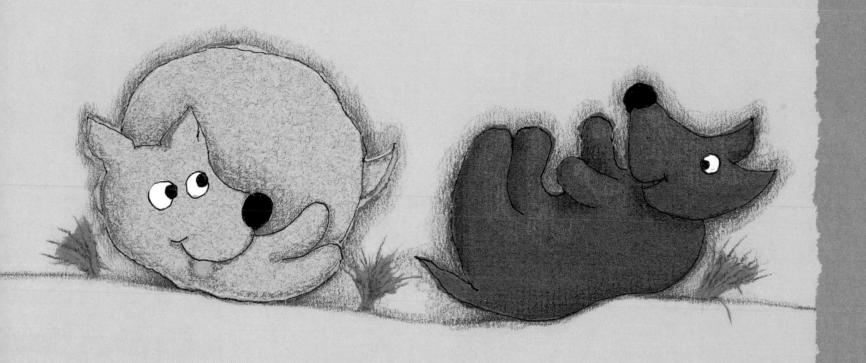

and round in the grass!

foal

Baby horses are called foals

and are very wobbly
on their legs.

baby mouse

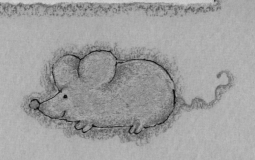

Some baby animals
are tiny, but others...

baby whale

aren't very small at all!